murmur

cameron barnett

murmur

cameron barnett

AUTUMN
HOUSE PRESS
Pittsburgh, PA

Cover Art by Melissa Dias-Mandoly
Book Design by Melissa Dias-Mandoly
Author Photo by Joshua Franzos

Library of Congress Cataloging-in-Publication Data

Names: Barnett, Cameron, author.
Title: Murmur / Cameron Barnett.
Other titles: Murmur (Compilation)
Description: Pittsburgh, PA : Autumn House Press, 2024. Identifiers: LCCN
 2023045756 (print) | LCCN 2023045757 (ebook) | ISBN
 9781637680872 (paperback) | ISBN 9781637680889 (epub)
Subjects: LCGFT: Poetry.
Classification: LCC PS3602.A77569 M87 2024 (print) | LCC PS3602.A77569
 (ebook) | DDC 811/.6--dc23/eng/20231002
LC record available at https://lccn.loc.gov/2023045756
LC ebook record available at https://lccn.loc.gov/2023045757

Autumn House Press is a nonprofit corporation
whose mission is the publication and promotion of
poetry and other fine literature. The press gratefully
acknowledges support from individual donors, pub-
lic and private foundations, and government agen-
cies. This book was supported, in part, by the Greater Pittsburgh Arts Council and the
Pennsylvania Council on the Arts, a state agency funded by the Commonwealth of
Pennsylvania, and the National Endowment for the Arts.

For Anna and for my family.

*"No, I can't feel your pain
but I can see the stars."*
—Saba

contents

I'm searching for the perfect light,

the perfect pen, the perfect place to loose an arrow
of forgiveness, neither forward nor backward, just true.

I'm searching for neither a true nor truer Blackness,
not for transformation without change,
not for the lingering scar but the scab long fallen off.

I'm searching, two fingers to the wrist, for whom
I tell myself to be, searching for love in an EKG,
searching for the murmur one decibel at a time.

I'm searching my messy truths for an arrhythmia
of remembrance, for a patriotism seven years sober
of supremacy, for a grammar of freedom precisely punctuated.

I'm searching for the crumbs I left behind without knowing,
for approval neither Black nor white, for the myth
of my making and the architect of my remaking,
for the muted laughter of ancestry breaking through.

A soft, indistinct sound

made by a person   *or group*

of people speaking quietly

all the glee

swept up between decades   echoes of good times

stuck   in hurricanes of laughter

mistaken for small winds

To make a low continuous sound

not every haunting is for horror   sometimes

it's just for company

A softly spoken   *or almost inaudible*   *utterance*

the book of my mother

and the book of my father   open   face-to-face

pages flipping past each other

To express one's discontent about (someone
or something) in a subdued manner

between who I am   and who I want to be

lies an earthquake

I cannot hold

The quiet or subdued expression

of a particular feeling   *by a group of people*

the redlining of my heart

≥

the minstrelsy of property value

To say something cautiously and discreetly

anywhere I go is an interracial space   a fun house

of mirrors

with all

the lights

turned off

Booker T.'s hand
stuffed into a boxing glove

A rumor

beneath the Atlantic

lies a massive aquifer

of fresh water   find me here

deep in all the water   you cannot see

To say something in a low

soft

or indistinct voice

as much as there are

seeds of truth

as much as there is

safe soil to hold them

as much as I am

my own sundown town

A recurring sound   heard in the heart through a stethoscope

that is usually a sign   of disease   or damage

languid lips dragging

over the chest

the cold cup of America

listening

Supreme

I dug beneath the court and I found
a blindfold, and I found its pain too.

I dug beneath the blindfold and I found
the roundness of eyes, and I found their pain too.

I dug beneath the eyes and I found
a woman, and I found her pain too.

I dug beneath the woman and I found
a wall, and I found its pain too.

I dug beneath the wall and I found
a noose, and I found its pain too.

I dug beneath the noose and I found
a branch, and I found its pain too.

I dug beneath the branch and I found
an arrowhead, and I found its pain too.

I dug beneath the arrowhead and I found
a home, and I found its pain too.

I dug beneath the home and I found
a love that loved me back, and I found its pain too.

I brought the love with me back up
to the surface, but I brought its pain too.

I held these things up in the air,
but people only stared and asked:

What right did I have to dig?

Murmur

This became my first ghost: the drum
of a stethoscope to my infant chest, an echo
deep in a doctor's ear, the sound she heard,
named it *murmur*—a swoosh in the space
between the beatings of my youngest heart

On the Ground

I was five on a fault line, back flat in bed,
shaken awake by a voice stretched long
across LA the first time the land spoke
to me. The lights above swung back
and forth across my eyes as I tried
to clutch whatever was closest,
fear welding my fingers into the bedsheets.
It was all over in moments. Listen
well enough and the earth will tell you
the quiet difference between a lie and history.
I walked out of my room to see my whole family
shaken and standing beneath a large crack
in the bent white ceiling of our living room,
and for a moment, I didn't know whether
what shook me had come from below or above;
my mother's midnight hands running through
my hair and her kiss on my cheek are the last
things I recall. Each time after, her touch of hair
or kiss of cheek was a retelling of that night,
a small *be careful* imprinted on the most vulnerable
part of me. Mothers will write whole histories
with their kisses, distracting us
from the fractures building within, and I wondered
when I might murmur myself apart, whether the
split would come from within or without, whether
my body's Black terrain would suffer subduction
to a 9 mm fault line in the dead of night sometime,
each kiss a reminder that I am a plundered land
pulled from Pangea, at constant risk to slip forever
beneath the force of another's—I've watched it now
more times than I care to count. You know, you can see
an earthquake coming if you know how to spot
a lie: the officer's bark, the hands, the lights swinging
madly over eyes, hands running rough over hair,
a murmur exploding in an instant—*get on the ground now!*
If you're not careful, you can become a quiet
history too. A subduction they'll call your fault.

I was made fingerprint first

so I would always know the price
of touch. I was made with a parapet septum;
when they passed a stud finder over it,
Mom's breath surfaced. I was made hot
in the blood and my God-knotted ghosts
nodded their heads in quorum. I've been on fire
ever since. My sister was made from the wink
of a lighthouse, my brother from a telescope
clapping in on itself. It's easy to forget
about your heart until you need it. I was made
unable to forget. I was made from the dirt.
Dad and I dig through the earth to find each other's
voices. I've been working on being worthy,
learning how to build such a man, and when
you found out, I gave it all my thought,
and when you learned my scheme, disapproval
escaped volcanic through your throat like the pop
of a soda can, and when I said I'd start over
that's when you learned to love me. I was made then too,
like the world itself—one tectonic tug at a time.

Corners

My love mentions that people see stars best
from the corners of their eyes, that cones
catch color in the centers, but it's the rods
on the outsides that fetch the dimmest portions
of the visible spectrum—and I must reconcile
with the fact that something as round
as vision still pushes people into corners

like those I pass in the hood, and wonder:
If spacetime had bent me a different path,
I could be a man or a mural on some concrete
patch like these, and that either way I could be
painted over eventually. I'm forced to consider

a future son, half white, and whether or not
to ever call him *my nigga*; that if I ever did,
something between us might break jagged
forever, pushed to the other sides
of rooms, a hypotenuse of hypotheticals
always between us. I'm forced to consider

my child's heart like a comma, caught up in clauses,
murmuring a steady syntax the way a ghost
drags its lips over every unspoken thing
caught in its chest, a soul full of expectations
never met. I'm reconciling how black and white
the edges of most things are, the steady strain

of looking into every corner of the sky and never
finding a Black constellation, already knowing
the brilliance of stars is a billion years' worth
of old news; reconciling with my friend

confessing he never expected to make it past
eighteen, and I don't know what's harder to believe:
his disclosure or the doctorate diploma he thumbs
on the corner of his thirties; reconciling

with people who hear my poems and come to me,
stumbling their way toward *I don't see color*—I can't
tell if it's glaucoma or Glaucon in their eyes
spinning the ring of Gyges, their mouths like a heart
pulsing so petulantly.

I take their hands to my chest, tap out
a sweet staccato: *Do you see me? Shut your eyes.*
Do you see me?

Little Africa on Fire

This is how the story begins: a touch, a bump, a hot mouth,
jostled skin in an elevator, escalation, tension, even just the illusion
of trespass. It always seems the smallest contact triggers the fire,
the tip of a match struck along the lips of containment.

~

For a while, my sister and I thought the world had no color
until the 1960s, convinced that old movies and photos were true
representations of history, whole stories; that color came
between cartoons and Civil Rights and long before then the world
was two-toned, light and dark, sometimes with flecks or aberrations
in the corners. Upon seeing pictures of our parents both black-
and-white and in color, we asked: *What changed?* Upon seeing pictures
of Greenwood, both beautiful and burned, I ask: *What stories
have I been taught to trust?*

~

There are three parts to a ghost story:
The Specter—planes in the sky,
dynamite dropped on a Black crowd,
a white mob, a machine gun expélling
bullets, American flag high behind it,
fire and smoke in its wake, a long march
past husks of burned-out churches,
eight days of interment of Blacks
by the thousands, loops of litigation
spraining the language of massacre into
"riot," insurance claims lost in the litter
of legal destruction.

~

The Apparition—a flat view of Earth
has always made Africa look little,
smaller than Greenland; a flat view
of Earth is what schools only had
for us to see ourselves; a flat view
of us pinned back prosecution and
punishment for the mapmakers,
cartographing themselves out
of the haunted history lying
flat beneath the earth.

The Murmur—we know a lie when it unfurls
in our hands, how consequences char
irregularity into myth; we know our hauntings
because a family keeps its ghosts close; we know
pain, we know plunder, we know echoes.

~

This is how to listen to a ghost story:
Remember that there are no better angels
above or beneath our skies, above or beneath
charred churches and trees. These angels,
their halos falling augustly, deciduously,
stories strapped to a branch lost against the forest.
Heaven is a Black place, a smoky silhouette
the tintype tattles on. Heaven is full of anomalies.
How do I explain my homesickness for this?
I can't stop dreaming about flames
in my mouth, in my palms and eyes at all times.
I can't stop crying for Tulsa and a hundred years
spent dirt-deep and silent beneath our feet.

~

This is how to cross-examine a ghost: Rouse it with radar
and listen to the echoes of old fire. Sometimes it takes a mouth
to pronounce what the earth has been whispering for generations.
sometimes flecks in the corners of photos are more
than aberrations, the black and white of it lying in plain sight.

~

This is how to give a ghost a home: Touch the dirt
outside your house and ask how different it might feel
in Greenwood, ask if the sunken anomalies push
against the surface around town, if those anomalies
still burn down deep, if the anomalies are still hot
in their mouths, their tongues boxes of un-struck matches.
It's the silence of fire that remains spectral, substituted
for memory—but no more. Little Africa pounds
heart-first against the dirt and emerges tongue, tooth,
and throat in bonfire, heritage unmortgaged,
a ghost-girl beating back the map of her unmaking.

South Carolina
March 2020

The land is an open mouth full of water. Even the rain
　　has nowhere to go. It sits and seeps by the road on the way
　　　　to the plantation I visit one night. Under a Chinese light show
I hold my love's white hand while we pass LED frogs and dragons.
　　I am not looking at the lights. I regard the live oaks
　　　　and what they might know—perhaps we recognize each other.
I didn't know how wooded this land was; I don't know everything
　　that these woods know, but I know the dark edges of the plantation
　　　　hold back everything I love. The pulse in my neck is a whisper
of wings through the branches. In the air, a barracoon tune hangs
　　like Spanish moss. In this, my making; in this, my heart. No joggling board
　　　　is flexible enough to bring together my tears and turf. From here, perhaps
I come, through a line of blacksmiths the census labeled "illiterate,"
　　and from illiteracy they come with the name Foggie hammered
　　　　into their blood, and from some other blood we know they were
purchased. I regard South Carolina as I do Ireland: two islands
　　in a sea of my becoming. Sometimes I wonder what else the land has
　　　　lied to me about. I wonder what the history books
would say if they knew how blood could echo. I wonder today,
　　as the news plays, what they expect me to think of distance—
　　　　as if this land hasn't been teaching it to me all along.

Murmur

When I'd run around as a toddler, my mother
always anticipated me falling down and not
getting back up. Later, my father's stethoscope
told us there was nothing there—this became
my second ghost

I'm not talking about the backyard

when my dad and I stand stoic,
    observing Virginia creeper cast itself up
        and down the trees of the property,
    the sweeping hill, three tiers slowly slipping
back into nature, and I say *I'm willing*
    to get in there and cut it all down. I'm not
        talking about the backyard when I tell him
    I want to take out each weed the steep slope
sprouts, clear brush, restore the switchback
    leading to the middle level before us. He's not talking
        about the backyard when, tenderly, he pushes back,
    says *not every vine needs to be chopped*, that *overgrown trees*
need only pruning, not topping. At the top, I see my sister
    lay out on a lawn chair letting the sun love her
        in ways she doesn't allow anything else to. She's always
    there but doesn't talk when Dad and I uncover
the curved masonry downhill, beautiful still, and imagine
    a fireplace or patio. I tell him I always wanted a fire
        to consume this space—he tells me he spent decades
    dreaming of something similar. We point and sweat
and slouch like seasoned workmen, imagining the paths
    and projects this hill can hold. We don't talk
        about the backyard to understand the promise
    only the trees see between us, the terraforming of years
we hope our hands might make. Predictions are nostalgia
    in reverse—we're talking about that when Dad finds
        a wet-winged butterfly on a stump he cut, lifts it
    with his finger while I hurl the shorn branches down
to the lowest level, and we take turns telling each other
    everything we'll do the day we finally get down there.

The Electrician

My grandfather
moved cargo
in the European theater
behind allied lines
to keep *our boys*
supplied

My grandfather
wired the island
of Okinawa
before America bombed
and broke
the whole nation

My grandfather
was honorably discharged
back to a broken nation
unwilling to rewire itself
for people like him

Worthy

                                        the cat comes
                from the other room   I know it is my skin
        he seeks   songs from the record player
            of my mind but
                            the needle does not orbit
                            only spins in place
        like the wooden block   beneath   ballerina toes
                                                I want to be worthy
        we have all come
        to make
        and to be made   even the gods
            workshop godliness   the ghost of my ghost
            slipping   into the seat left warm   for me   a second spoon
                    tucked tightly   next to the first   the coffee
        croissants and company   outside   the snowstorm they called for
                                                now calling us   how
                        to make the metaphor
                        to do the gesture but withhold   the movement
        the ghost slips sugar over
            the lip of the mug   silence
                                            has begun sending out invitations
        clanking typing tapping reading   each of us has
                                    a poem in our hearts
                        to share   words
        worn as laurels   in this silence   hallowed be
                                thy name
                                            the past slipping
                                                    the ghost's lips
            a mirror that does not reflect
            but refracts   the second spoon caught
        by the first's shadow
                        utility bound by futility   how to make   I shouldn't

draw lines

                such that make an architect   crumple

sometimes just enough

                       of the world

is too much   too much blood   for the pump

            too much snow   for the shovel's throat

            too much weight   too much of me

                       in me to carry

                       but I must

    am I not   worthy? are we not all

                       gods working to be?

Stop Me

If I ever met the president, you might
have to stop me from calling him

a nigger—reparations: I don't trust people
who speak simply about complex things—

kid wisdom: the floor is always lava, don't step
on the cracks in sidewalks—superstition:

a ghost story is a conjuring, not a burial—
witness: the twine it takes a sycamore

to still a Black body—silence: if I ever met
the president, it wouldn't be a question

whose button is bigger, his red and mine BLACK
LIVES MATTER—take a knee: I sit in the back

of a poetry reading and notice all the funny things
that necks do—predictable: I stand for the anthem

and notice all the funny things people do
to remind themselves they love something—

desperation: sometimes a recipe can be too
literal—knuckle blood: bigotry wears the same dress

to every party, dances the same tired
dance—lonely: I'm no good—lonely: I'm

no good without a good drink and a murder
of white women flocking by—ghost story:

stop me if this sounds familiar to anybody,
I'm no tissue for drying your racism—thin:

the property line between a blessing and—a privilege:
if we ever meet, I'd have to tell you that we have

no *better angels*—privilege: all my windows
and mirrors are beginning to look the same—

stop me: first place in a swim meet in a sewer—politics:
if I ever met the president (yuge, hubris, hyperbole),

if I ever met the president—stop me: if I ever met
the president, I'd remind him about the funny thing

necks do between twine—witness: if I ever met
the president I'd be no good without a ghost—story:

all the funny things bigotry does backlit with—
gaslighting: when I take a knee it's for the undoing

of knots around the necks of my ancestors—rewind:
if my neck ever does something funny, stop me; if I ever

step on the cracks, stop me; if I am ever murdered
by a white woman, stop me; if I ever introduce myself

as a ghost story, stop me; if I ever call the president
a nigger—silence.

Vital Signs

There is a point when nourishment tilts toward poisoning,
that despite all good intention, what we feed ourselves can bypass
whole systems; a point when you can only listen
to your history if you've learned not to fear voices.

I learn that in Khmer they say, *The water in my heart has fallen*,
because there is no direct word for depression, and I realize
I am at the point where speaking directly chasms my meaning.

In running, there is a point when you begin to question why
you began in the first place, when your feet are concrete
metronomes, when your heart wants to split your chest
Alien-style; how clear the importance of pulse and protection.

There is a point when you have to choose what to believe in.
I've been writing redactions of myself one by one, blacking out
everything inflammatory, the charring fiction of history building up
between the layer of myself and my second-self conversing
across the divide of fallen water, pointing fingers at the liar.

There is a point in watching death when the body becomes nothing
more than a body. There is a point when you begin to wonder
if the essence has left yet or if it's standing among the rest of the crowd.
There is a point when the silence of ghosts becomes a lesson.

Ghost Lessons

My great-great-great-grandmother
    stares at me in sepia. We both stand
in our own classrooms. History has
    a funny way of being a hallway,
an isthmus, a ██,or sometimes a thimble
    covering what hopes to avoid piercing.
How do you hold a family together?
    Pin this: Portia would flourish her hands

in bid whist to show off "her friends," diamonds
    on different fingers. What hands can
hold is often all that's passed on, often ██. My grandmothers
    pulled thread through Pittsburgh, master
seamstresses, their hands stitching steel through cloth, white-
    passing palms and pulses soft beneath skin,
which can be a thimble itself if you let the pinpricks

    and ██ teach you. I have learned
teaching is a thing of the blood. Dad
    taught me when to tuck my tongue
in my pocket, when to listen. When they speak,
    my elders drop a's from days so that it's
Mondy, Tuesdy, Wednesdy—ancestry
    is one giant game of telephone echoed
through tin can decades. Pin this: Porky

    hiding happiness deep in his dimples. Pin this: Spoogie
and Pidgeon took the yellow boat out in LA
    and the sea nearly took them. A name is a story,
and Dad taught me not to tell all my stories
    at once—then we both forgot. I remind myself
there's ██ in remembrance, a heaven
    all around me: A ghost of mine is colorblind when it looks
out at the world; a ghost of mine is colorblind

when it looks at itself. What right do I have to play
the prism? My matriarchs pulled legacy
    through eyes of steel and still so many people
in my family have tried or failed or succeeded
    at leaving this land. Sometimes I almost believe
I understand. Pin this: The Barnetts backstitched
    love into this land to make sure I'd always
feel held, even when I knit negativity out

    of whole cloth, or search for purpose
in my pinpricks. My grandmothers
    knew needles pull more than thread;
I'm searching their patterns for all the lessons
    of ancestry left behind—How to
mend your heart: ██. How to be a better man: ██.
How to be Black: ██. How Black
to be: ██ How to write the story of yourself:
██████████ .

Murmur

I played every sport I could growing up. I ran
until no kid in my class could outpace me.
I beat my heart up and down playgrounds and courts,
through grass stains and bloody knees. I wanted
to learn how to make my heart sing, and I wanted
to silence it too, but always my mother's gaze
pressed heavy on me

Ones and Zeros

0.

I wanted to write something
quaint and coded, but all
I could manage
was the letter
"I" on one side
of a page.

1.

When
I was younger
I never felt whole,
I only felt my
divisions.

0.

If the body were a sentence,
would we place the heart
behind an ampersand
or between brackets?

0.

When
I was younger,
I learned that a rainbow
is just a trick, a kiss
of light and water. When
I was younger,
I stopped giving
kisses for fear
of being tricked.

1.

The big bang is, after all,
just another theory, and
theory is where we all begin.

0.

Anymore, we're too busy
listing fears as ones and zeros
on the internet, an infinity
of digits weighing us down.

0.

It's no wonder
I find my best
reflection toward
the margins
of most things.

1.

If the body is just a trick,
a collective nothingness,
quaint and coded, all ones
and zeros, then it's no wonder
I never felt whole
until you kissed me.

Breath

What I'm saying is blood was never blue, never
      neatly distinguished nor diagrammed.
What I'm saying is that Newton's third law states
      every prayer has an equal and opposite curse.
What I'm saying is that all our hearts once held
      trapdoors that helped us slip past suffocation, but
a trapdoor can only be a trap once—hallelujah.
      You were your mother's blood, her body, and yes,
her breath. You carry the scar of her love, or
      as Newton suggests, her pain, too. The heart
is the only organ we describe with chambers,
      a place of meeting rooms meant for
not meeting. What I'm saying is there was a time
      we all broke the rules—they want you to forget
your first breaths passed through your mother's lips—
      they want you to fall through trapdoors and
disappear umbilically. Be it red or blue, your blood
      is an allograph of inhalation, a synonym, a murmur.
What I'm saying is your last breath is the curse
      of your first, that all the letters of your alphabet
belong to the wind and your mother's wishes, lies,
      and dreams slipped between the chambers
of your heart because, whether broken or whole,
      a promise is an allograph of betrayal—Newton said it
himself—that's just science, and the math is clear
      that our infant hearts have a word problem
hair-triggered and primed to slip out beneath us,
      and by us, I mean them, who you told me is we,
and I only know that this heartbeat of mine
      is a simple, persistent knock on the door asking
to be let in, to be let out, to be let in again.

Twenty Eight Teen

I've been feeling less canvas and more easel.
I eat only to realize I am being eaten.
I am guilty on thirty-two counts of teeth
collecting nothing but welfare and plaque. First

my bite, then my bark. I wish for you
a misdemeanor of memories so arresting
the clench of wrists behind back stops your heart.
But you keep on beating. You keep on—you keep

on keeping space for space's sake, or birthright,
and I've been feeling like a clock of bones clacking
beneath the dirt; I've been feeling like lumber
fish-scaled from fire; I've been feeling on fire

as I watch you drop cream into coffee to cut
its strength and grind me down into the blackest
grounds. I wish that was the end of it. I wish
for you a toilet with no drain, or a fuck-you poem

that keeps fucking you up the way a lie
fills a body with helium then cuts the string.
Listen: I've been feeling forty-five in my neck
and eighteen in my fists, and I'm just a few months

shy of taking years off your life, or your pension,
or your prescription for bitching and whining about all
the power your hands hold but never feel. The piss
in your pot is brighter than most of my days.

Your word for this is *justice*. My word for this is *cutlery*.
Know this: You can't make chicken soup
out of chicken shit, and I've been feeling like a chef
with no ingredients but a lifetime of recipes.

To eat without being eaten. I'm not asking—I'm telling.

Reading Black Poems to White Audiences:
A How-to Guide

Part III: The N-Word

. . . Nigga, say nigga all the time
Say nigga to the left, and nigga to the right
Say nigga like you're playing Simon Says
and you can't move unless somebody says nigga
Say nigga to the old lady in the front like you're spilling some big secret
Say nigga to the old man in the back like you just spilled his big ass secret
Say nigga top to bottom like you patting down the audience
before you let them hear the rest of the poem
Say nigga like you're counting jumping jacks—one nigga, two nigga, three
     nigga, four . . .
Say it to the ceiling like you want the roof to hear it
and if the roof ain't listening say it to the floor
like you want your dead homie to hear it down below
Then say nigga as if your dead homie down there came back
and you only get one word to share with him
Say nigga till your bones get hot
Say nigga like you're making a bonfire
Say nigga like you're starting a fire
with nothing but the bones of dead homies
Say nigga like rain on a roof, the one that ain't listening
Say nigga to the twelve-year-old who ain't looking at you
'cause his phone is in the way and say nigga to his father
who's thinking twice about bringing his kid to your reading
And once you've said nigga to every white person in the room,
say nigga to the only other nigga there
the way you'd tell your mother you love her
And don't be alarmed when the well-meaning man in his seventies
says to you "your poems are good but I'm just tired of Black poets
making me feel bad about slavery and Jim Crow"
Remember, he's "well-meaning"—help him feel Jim Crow another way—
invite him up to the mic—help him feel slavery like he hasn't
felt it before—wrap the cord over his shoulders,
down his collar, loop it like a necktie and dangle it
by his mouth then say it with him—*nigga*—and if he hesitates

pull the cord tighter and say it with him—*nigga*—and if he stammers
loop the cord again and whisper in his ear—*nigga*—and if he squirms
pull the cord tighter till he says it, tighter still until he feels it
in his bones—*nigga*—and when he gets hot enough
start a fire, nigga

Black Holes

Consider the body. Consider the pulse and pump and thump of life within. You are, in a sense, a sentient sack of plumbing. Consider the body cavernous—a video I watch asks, "How many holes does a human have?" and it turns out we are not the donut we are so often colloquialized to be. A jar, a cup, a bowl, a plate—holes only exist if there is a body to host it—the paradox of containment. In the video, I learn that openings aren't holes, just parts of holes—that a straw is one thing with two parts. Consider Blackness. Consider the body black—the whole of it sucked through the kinked straw of history, opening to opening. Consider how whole lives were squeezed out of Black bodies. Consider the ancestors who prayed for shipwreck, who prayed to be flooded in order to be freed. Consider the weight of what's been kept inside the spaces of our bodies in order to make it. Consider the spaces where our bodies hide, that visibility and invisibility are the same weight double-stacked on Blackness. Consider the weight of black holes—supermassive ghosts who lurk dark in deep space. They say at the event horizon, a body sucked in would stay frozen in time forever. Not every hole has an exit. Consider chambers and dead ends and their singular openings. Consider Black descendants praying for singularity in order to be free of space and time's cruelties. Physicists consider this point so dense that the laws of physics as we know them break down. Black people might not consider this such a bad thing—how long have we prayed for a different physics? Were it not for gravity we would bend the world holy. As it turns out, gravity is the weakest force the universe has to offer. As it turns out, the physicists are silent on the force of justice. Not even a consideration. Consider Blackness, supermassive and free of gravity, bending the arc of the moral universe all the way around until it's whole.

Murmur

Be careful she would say, and *Be careful* Dad would say.
I ignored them. When I did karate in high school,
squaring up against men twice my size, my mother said
Be careful and my father said *Be smart* and because
I didn't care for my heart then, I was careless

Kamehameha

I'm still not convinced I can't be Goku. All I want
is to protect my people. Since thirteen I've been trying;
sometimes I, too, crouch in a rage and scream galactically
to feel a bit of power. I don't have an orange suit though,

I don't have a tail (that I know of), I don't have a Kinto'un
to catch me when I fall, but still I'm not convinced
I couldn't walk out of work, hold my hands up
to the sky for hours and slowly cull together enough spirit

to blow down a city clean flat. But I have to be honest:
My friends call me Krillin because sometimes I care
too much, or take a beating I know I can't withstand,
or fall for people who only seem human—but all I want

is to protect my people, and there are no senzu beans
for keeping us alive. I'm not convinced I know where
I come from. Neither did Goku but that didn't stop him
from going Super Saiyan. Isn't it alien to find so much power

within yourself that the whole world considers it a myth?
It might sound weird, but what Black boy hasn't
walked through the heart of America and wondered
if he was from another planet? It might sound weird,

but I'm not the only Black boy who has taken a stance—*KA*—
in his room, hands pinned to hip—*ME*—calling a blue orb
into being—*HA*—between his palms—*ME*—then fired—*HA*!

On Finding Love in Unanticipated Moments, or My Father Gives Me a Shirt His Father Gave Him Before He Died

What we call sight is just a sliver of a spectrum. Today, we'd call the shirt unsightly. When he called me over, I knew Grandpa's heartfelt gift was given when Dad was my age—the age just before his father's passing, of which he'd rarely speak.

I never said I knew death, but I knew my father's haunted heart: Weight passed on, his emptying, his hand a bowl breaking into a spoon, the hollowing out of one closet of things into the next. I named his unstitched shadow without even speaking.

I was eleven years old. It was long hidden in a closet. I cannot tell you whether we sat or stood, but I need you to know this isn't a black or white thing; I need you to know my Peter Pan heart. I accepted it without even speaking,

a gift from his father: sixties short sleeve button down, way-wide collar points running isosceles toward the armpits, complete with a swirl of browns, greens, oranges, and yellows loud enough to speak.

Where does a father begin? I never mentioned love, never mentioned air. His shirt hung heavy between hoodies and suits as I slept; dreams of my father and his father and me, all our hearts ghosting without speaking

the word *death* at all. Because I was too young, I sobbed; my father must have too, once. I knew it by how he came back to my bed as if to thread back what was already leaving me behind. I hadn't learned why a person would speak even

without understanding themselves. His soothing touch . . . I didn't know which of us it was for. Where does a grandfather end? A bit of the boy died in me then, another Barnett hollowed by a love unanticipated but asked for without even speaking.

My father cupped me in his arms—I never said he couldn't hold everything in, never said he couldn't look at me like the ghost of a boy he knew deeply, sliver of something sacred, tell me *everything will be alright, Cameron* without even speaking.

Swisshelm Park

It's easy to love what's easily missed:
If this elbow of the city could bend itself
open, loose with the weight of its history,
loose with Commercial's long wind
like an umbilical cord, loose with Whipple's
steep sloping into Edgewood, you might feel
the flex of the Monongahela passing by, a figure eight
of homes, rows of neighbors, the hum
of some distant freight moving through the night,
and you might feel the amenity afforded
by this place—the small delight of being forgotten.

It's easy to love what's easily missed:
the air-raid siren wailing long into a new millennium,
a highway screaming by, a river sleuthing out
this semi-suburb, well-known woods wrapping
themselves around the neck of the neighborhood,
my childhood bike doing loops around the low and long hills
of concrete, tire tracks of a third-generation boy
scraped into the blacktop, third iteration of integration
into the neighborhood, home in the crook
of the road, home by an island in the road, island
sprouting a lone tree, the tree rising taller with
each generation, centuries seeded and ceded
by the Susquehannock, who take
no small delight in being forgotten.

It's easy to love what's easily missed:
the space between vale and helm razor thin
but deep cut by borough and court claim,
land divided and sold for summer homes
on the old farmland of Jane the abolitionist,
who taught and fought for women, who fed
and hid freedom-seeking people, the Underground
Railroad being the first trains to station here before
steel and slag and industry dusted over the sleepy
cul-de-sacs and dead ends—easy to love. Easy
to miss all the life you pass by on your commute,

all the history these congested tunnels plunge through,
all our small delights cooped and cupped up
in the bent arms of embrace—hard to be forgotten.

VY CMa

1.

Here's a short story: Contraction leaves me breathless. On a mountain, my lungs are bags of magma. I wonder about falling. Am I 100 percent of anything? There is a river right in front of me, and I am the mountain. A bicycle. A stop sign. Shade shifting with the wind. I spot an old friend who has taught me about this. She is a graduate today. In the picture, my body is showing all the warning signs of eruption. This, too, she has taught me to control. I hug her on the perimeter. I don't want her to know how hard I fall.

Afterthought: The motion of a hinge is its own undoing. Imagine all the doors you know failing all at once, the awful sound of that letdown. I've always loved revolving doors for this reason: to know when you're entering and when you're exiting. A passing in and out in one motion. The body I was born with is a collection of hinges. Yes, the heart. Yes, the spirit. Yes, the mind. I have broken both of my arms at separate, key times in my life—being flexible isn't a novelty, it is survival.

2.

Here's a long story: I would need another lifetime to tell you everything I want to tell you about this one. I would need another still to do most of what I'd like to do in the first. I won't say that time is a revolving door. The body I was born with has gravity, has light, has orbit. These are not my favorite parts of it. A body is most interesting where it bends—this is where the potential for collapse lies. I'm learning to embrace all the places where my body fails me.

Afterthought: The largest star ever observed by man is thousands of times larger than our sun. This puts me in harmony with the dust. I imagine a wall of fire so large that even bending backward isn't enough to see the top of it. I imagine what a lonely song it must sing. I've heard that solar flares have a sound. I think of this at night with my head on the pillow, the slosh of blood echoing through it and back to my ear. I fall asleep assuming everything in the universe has a high and low tide.

3.

Calculations		
60 min x 24 hours = 1,440 min/day *1,440 min/day x 365 days =* *525,600 mins/year*	If time and space are one and the same then I am the Golden Record of Voyager 1—love with velocity	
math is not my strength, but it is required for every race; survival and leisure	*525,600 min/year ÷ 9 min/mile =* *58,400 miles/year (Average speed)*	
R1 VY CMa = *614,378,620 mi x 2 =* *1,228,757,240 mi* *(Diameter)*	are equal parts pulse and calculation	*R2 VY CMa =* *614,101,147 mi x 2 =* *1,228,202,294 mi* *(Diameter)*
the way around anything is irrational— when the lungs	*Max Circumference = π x* *1,228,757,240 mi =* *3,860,254,718 mi* *OR* *Min Circumference = π x* *1,228,202,294 mi =* *3,858,511,304 mi*	are burning from breath, deep breathing is the effective solution
MaxC VY CMa ÷ *Average Speed =* *66,100.25 years* *Years on VY CMa ÷* *years per life (79.05) =* *836.18 lives*	there are names I have gone by that I have never known—a small or smaller black mark, the real and the perceived	*MinC VY CMa ÷* *Average Speed =* *66,070.39 years* *Years on VY CMa ÷* *years per life (79.05) =* *835.80 lives*
the needle on the Golden Record must be dull by now; a song always rubs against its singer—a thread in search of scissors.		

4.

How many forevers do I have to spare?
        It begins as so many other things do: on the outside.
    A rolling in. The first strike intended
        to be on the perimeter. A hinging. Contraction,
lengthening, relaxation. Everywhere we go,
        we are falling. The body is not its own master.
    It is subject to pulling. To push against this, it must
        pull itself. I am faster than most people I know. Perhaps
this means I am falling more than they are. Do I have
        less control? There is too much debate on who is wrong
and who is right about something so ordinary.
        Our ancestors would have laughed
            at the way we carry ourselves.
        (Not a laugh but a shudder; not a shudder
            but a gasp; not a gasp but a choking.
                (Not a debate but a shudder; not a shudder
                    but an itch; not an itch but an alerting.))

5.

There is already too much in my life
that is constantly bending. But this
is my addiction. Bring me to my knees.
I want to kiss the ground. There are places
this is impossible, and those are where
I want to be, or where I want to die, or
at least try. Today they said water
is flowing on Mars. My own list
of impossibilities is a mile shorter
than it was yesterday, and yesterday
seems a mile shorter than it ever was,
and a mile is the length of the seam
running down my jeans. My patella
is a turtle shell, a body that hides water
but barely bends. Mars may be a red turtle,
but my eye has gone canine. With more
time, I would conquer the greater dog
in the sky. If I can't have water,
I will have fire instead.

6.

The Earth's circumference is 24,901 miles.
I could round it in under half a year—
155.6 days. Between the greater dog

and the Earth, a ratio of 1:28,171. Our Sun
can hold over 1,000,000 Earths, they say.
If the Sun were the parent of our solar system,

would we be its favorite child? What parent wants
such a troublemaker—but still there is pride
in chasing. There was a time when it was nothing

to sprint through an afternoon in the front yard
where Dylan would skateboard and Afton was deep
in the dirt, picking worms or scooping up Dad's sawdust.

I had strong legs. I had just one broken arm.
Southern California would never let go of summer,
even as I chased it around the block.

When I threw a rock in the well in my neighbor's yard,
both the well and the water began to disappear;
I was afraid I had broken too much.

7.

KG asks me *Wouldn't time be different
on the star, from the sheer size?* and I
begin to squeeze my knees. It isn't a black
hole, but the imminence of collapse
has me swollen. I tell them if it sat
where our sun sits, its surface
would extend past the orbit of Jupiter.

At 6 o'clock we're eating Twix bars
and consoling each other. At 6:01—
the sugar rush, dead sprint through veins.
Contraction is at the heart of it all.
Soon, KG is grabbing their knees too.
I double-check my math to be sure
we'd have the same number of lifetimes
on the star together. My body fails me
when I read the calculations.

What would Galileo have thought
if he saw me up there? Would he admire
my dorsiflexion? Would he ogle
any buckle in my knees, or swoon
at the swaying of my hamstrings, maybe
press his eye too hard into the telescope.
All the blood wouldn't come close
to the red of this monster in the sky that I love.

I don't tell KG that their question
shrinks me more than the greater dog
itself. Equal and opposite reaction.
The way my calf comes to kiss
its nearest flesh. This is my undoing.
Between hip and ankle, a star
is spinning.

8.

Here's the story: On Wednesday I was homesick
for a place so faraway, the distance measured
in parsecs, thousands of them. Then, an itch
in my throat, a hum of blood, the heart as a red dwarf.
Here's the story: Everything we send into space
is a pyramid. Bury me in one and point it
just past Pluto. Space isn't an ocean; I am
no Magellan. I'm not planting a flag, I am opening
a door, I am fraying neatly tied ends, I am undoing
this distance—how many generations it takes
to achieve your dream. Then, a twitch behind
the patella, a yearning in the calf, the retrograde
motion of collapse. Who is sure the whole universe
isn't stumbling? I want badly to believe in limits.
Here's the story: negative chemistry. Dark matter
in the blood. I fear paralysis above all else. If I don't
subdue the dog, who will? A lifetime is a finite thing
to waste; an eruption of the heart is a sorry thing
to miss. Today, my heavy breathing leaves me
just shy of the sky I used to look toward
with a broken arm, the three-eyed stare of Orion's
Belt looming down, half challenge, half intimidation.
Tomorrow I will be at the equator, feet on either
hemisphere, lungs breathing summer and winter,
the hinging synced to the beat of the seasons,
the planet still bringing me to my knees.

Murmur

Heartbreak came when I fell in love for the first time,
and my mother said nothing and my father said nothing,
and years passed with no echo to interrupt the ending,
as they held me, and we all listened to my third ghost
singing in the space between heartbeats

The Pipe Bearer

How do you change the world? A slow soak of oil—history is   like that, and a glance finds so much familiar. A century of new hues   slathered onto wood. That's process—take a second look: staff in   hand,   white power clenched, clean jaw of Black youth tilted, and   race   breaks di- agonal between them (progress). Take a second   look. A semblance of symmetry saved by the far corner. East could   be anywhere as long as it's not here. Would that he say something   of lips and their lies. Now that's radical. A brushstroke is process;   what's left behind is (prog- ress). So hard not to confuse object   and subject. Take a second to look. Would that the jambiya slip   its scabbard to cut off the breath, the   paternal   posturing—are   both not pretenders? Stare meets pro- cess meets progress meets de-   viation. Both sets of eyes to the west, some south   of   shame,   some   south of skepticism and hope—one brings, another consumes rad-   ically, the old gold frame holding it together, but its cracks betray   the breaking. How else do you change the world? It takes a second to   look. East is not anywhere centered. Radical, indirect, emotionless   gazes. What would the pipe say of this voyeurism in garb and   grasp,   of the failure to grasp the Blackness before him? That ain't radical.   Would that the walls fail, the pipe tumble, the eyes level and meet   to see what's really there.

New Fruit Humming

I'm here to say sorry.
Because you definitely said splotchy.
Because I definitely heard splotchy,
because I definitely told everyone about
how you said splotchy with your eyes cast down,
and everyone said "Ain't that some shit!" because
who the hell talks about their kids like that?
So I'm here to say sorry. Because I didn't
stay silent, and what I really said was,
"I know . . . " or "Yeah . . . " and took a bite
of the pear in my hand because we were under
an apple tree and you brought pears, and I thought
"How strange is this?" never doubting the taste
in my mouth, never doubting what I tasted
wasn't the flesh of the fruit, never admitting that
to you because compromise tasted like oranges
so we just lied and lied and lied, and I've lied
about this story before. We weren't in bed
because we were definitely under an apple tree
as much as an apple tree can be a bed, and
it was definitely hotter than August though the sun
said April, and you said "It just worries me,"
and now I'm here to say sorry. Because I was
wrong to believe you were afraid of anything,
because my Blackness wasn't anything
to be afraid of, because my Blackness wasn't anything
to you. I don't tell people we were under a tree because
a bed is a better place to lie, or a better place to lay,
because I still mix up laying and lying, because the story
is still so mixed up I don't know if it even matters
because forgiveness is an act of retelling,
and forgiveness is an act of retelling,
and forgiveness is an act of retelling.
When I think back on that day, I start to cry
not because I'm sad, but because my left eye
and my right eye can't put you together and it hurts
to try because you were so mixed up, because
you were so afraid of us mixing, and that's why
we were under a tree and not in a bed, and that's
why my Blackness is afraid of nothing, and that's

why it's so hard to lie sometimes (I loved you),
and I'd be lying if I said I'm sorry (you loved me)
and now there's new fruit humming
in the old fruit tree.

Getting to the Party
for Greg

1.

Before a flight to Los Angeles
my mother texts me the results
of her 23andMe test, says *Keep this
just to us.* The evidence: 52.8%
European, 44.5% Sub-Saharan African.
I elbow my coworker next to me,
tip the phone screen into her laughter,
the kind of Black woman laughter that can't be
replicated in a lab, that fills the fuselage
from the plane's tail up—beneath us the clouds
look curdled, and the world turns triangular.

2.

Maybe there is laughter in our DNA
that we bury down deep. Why else
do we laugh? How else could we?

3.

Somewhere, there's a party we are always trying
to get to, all of us searching for *that* music, for *those*
people, for good vibes vibrating all over
and under our skin. There's a party
I'm trying to get to where I am 100%
of something, skin to cell. Most days
I move through the world dreaming
of the party—*the one party*—the coming-
of-age moment forever furloughed
into an untested future.

4.

When I text my mother back I don't say
what I mean. I send a *haha*, a laughter
inadequate in any space. I send a quip about
understanding who I am, which is laughable
in this moment. What I don't send: my tears,
my wildest heart, the torn self of my twenties,
the trepidation of being a living hypocrisy
no matter what I say. In this moment I can only
laugh—what else could there be in me?

5.

There's a party I keep dreaming of, unscratched
vinyl spinning on a raised platform. I dream
my cells are a laugh track, the room all faces, audience,
actors, and props. This is *the* party, *the one*. Haven't I
arrived? It's what my dream skin tells me, which
in the dream is every color and no color all at once.
I'm never speaking in the dream. At the party
my fingers go vinyl, my nostalgia goes primal,
and I go looking for hope in the corners
of words. The crowd comes into sharp focus.
The faces; the skin; the room turns triangular.

6.

Sometimes I have a bad habit
of not telling the people I love
what I really mean.
> *It was a company that stripped ancestry*
> *from our family in the first place,*
> *why pay thieves for an itemized receipt*
> *of their plunder?*
Sometimes I have a bad habit
of not really meaning what I tell
the people I love.
> *Haha.*

7.

There's a dream I dare to have of finding all the cool kids
I looked up to as a teen gathered at the party, clean
coiffed in Nikes and Livestrong bracelets, ripped jeans
rubbing against almond-milk skin. There's a dream
I dare to have with party guests of every person
who has ever told me *You're so white* and I'd raise
a glass to them and toast them for being *So right*
and we'd offer each other daps, handshakes,
high fives, and other microscopic congratulations
skin-to-skin. This is my party—the problem is
the past: You actually have to miss something
to feel it.

8.

When the plane lands I step back out into the land
of my birth. The land and my ancestry share a history
of being stolen. In the heat I lace up my Nikes
and plod a path through the fresh fragrance of oranges
laced along the neighborhood's branches. I think
of my father, the most nostalgic man, and recall his
toil in our yard every season, rearranging his dreams
like strips of lawn rolled out all around our home
and recall the heat in each strip of my skin.

9.

There's a dream I keep wanting to have of losing control
of myself, wistful for good times with bad people, wistful
for a wet eye and a full pen. I eye the word "Sub-Saharan"
and think *I can know* how *Black and never know* what *Black.*
There's a morning I keep hoping for when I wake up
after a party that never was, realizing the world doesn't spin
but bounces between the same three points.
There's longing for who I am right now that I keep
wanting to have; there's a longing for the generation
before the generation before me; there's a longing
for the laughter of a continent I've never stood on;
there's a party we are all trying to triangulate, an ancestor's
wild dream we're all trying to see ourselves in, a DNA
that doesn't laugh in our faces.

Clotilda

Charred wreck of old white men's bets—say it with me: America
finds itself in the muck once again. I read about the dinosaur-spined
schooner scuttled in the silt of Mobile, and my body bends

to the language of this loss, all vex and reflex. 'Least they know, I think
to myself. I think: Somewhere a MAGA-minded son of the South reads
about the last slave ship to bring Africans to America, jokes

about a return trip back to Benin. 'Least we know how this ends—
say it with me: states' rights, Southern way, Calloo-Callay, no work today.
'Least we know this is where it stopped, don't we? My mind is muddied

reading about this cenotaph choked back from the past, the almost
immediate overtures for research and Reconstruction, and I must
resolve to think to myself, Hey, 'least we know who did it though,

right? 'Least they know the dimensions. 86' x 23' they measure
with tape, but my blood knows the true size of a ship is displacement,
knows the size of slavery isn't feet but fear, the beam of generations

forever shackled to the delta, and I'm supposed to celebrate
another dinosaur the dirt coughed up like America isn't already
a museum of natural history back-braced with the bones

of twenty generations of Clotildas. 'Least they know Cudjo.
'Least they know the slavers were caught and never charged.
'Least we're used to that a hundred and sixty years past the trafficking.

'Least they knew where to look from Foster's written records.
No surprise here. Isn't it just like the acquitted to brag and confess their work:
Zimmerman, Wilson, Shelby, Pantaleo, Yanez. 'Least they know there's money

in it. Always the profit, even in the water, even in the archaeology, even
in their excitement, even in their excavation. A slave ship sails back and
all they can say is *Maybe*—even now, that's just the least they know.

Working for the City

That's what we used to call it
                back then
            my cousin tells me (deep
                    leaning
            into chair and memory)
                    of Blacks
                        who dated whites

and I want to say

                        to no one in particular

So call me Comptroller   call me
        Commissioner
                        call me Fire Chief
        and I will handle
            all
            the heat
                you heave   Tomorrow I'll be Public
                Works Director   because a hole
                    is in my heart—the more
                        it is filled
                        the deeper
                        it grows until
                        I am hollow
                        entirely

The next day
                    elect me Mayor
                            just to watch me
                    apologize for things
            I can't apologize for

                        I'm sorry I love my city

I'm sorry I can never
turn my back on her

Skipping Stones to Andromeda

       you drag   the very space   around you
into you   a magnet   attracted
      to itself   the only way
left that I know   to send love
is to skip   a stone   it seems
         you and I are two
galaxies that don't know   we are
         destined to crash   into each other
letting our   stars spin   madly
through space   each of us missing
      the black holes that lie   at the other's center
sometimes   it is easy to forget
      the great weight at our cores   my heart
spinning like a pulsar   your heart   shrouded
in nebula   all you see of me   blips of
light in a cloudy darkness   a light-year
     just a stone's throw through space
and still   it seems   I am the only thing
    escaping your gravity

Pericardium

A friend reminds me that a pulse is worth believing in;
Mother feels the advice sink in miles away, whispers *this*

had better hold. I don't begrudge her prayers—to give the world
a child with no safety nets designed for him, only a cat's cradle of

son and survival, tangled thread. What could be more broken?
A space exists between heartbeats especially vulnerable to fatal misfire;

son and father meet here, our shadows holding hands, squeezing some.
Who would have thought? Lacuna matata. May we never forget mothers

grew big with windows and mirrors for us to break into telescopes, to live
into our hearts' deep paradiddles and electric logarithms. We need only

the murmur of ribs among one another to remember. We need only listen to
echoes of the cracked spine of unrequited history speaking of what to bury:

of long ghosts and their misfires; of a blood and bones
manhood.

If my blood never sleeps

it's because my cousin always says *Pray by moving*
    your feet, fitting as he hikes mountains in arid places
        far from where he began. My cousin always says *Be*
a fountain, not a drain, a play on a family name.
    My cousin sails Caribbean waters like a long prayer
        in his heart and so I've taken his advice to mine.
I move my feet almost always for sport or blood
    or distance, for praise from ghosts of my making,
        their feet long moved for freedom, their footsteps
left lurking in the corners of plain sight. Some blood
    is made for bleeding. I'm convinced if a footstep is a prayer,
        then America is a church of benedictions and blasphemies
enough to stuff a bible. My cousin is always moving
    his feet, and blood always moves mine because blood
        never sleeps. It prays in diastolics, every pulse a pace,
every step a signal to specters with spent stomachs
    and mouthfuls of stories, and the chapters are titled *Dakota, Carolina,*
        Virginia, Saskatchewan, Boston, Pittsburgh, where I sit and write words
so many million prayers away from the land of my birth
    because America is a wide church, and the aisles are not marble,
        but rows of myth and myopathy, and treading too hard will wake
the wrong ghosts so sometimes I just sit. Sometimes I wonder
    whether I am the fountain or the drain of generations to come.
        I've prayed my way to a census of the dead to understand how I
am alive, and this is how the game goes—a long jumper
    in the sport of self-knowing who can't tell you the score.
        I feel my feet beginning to fall asleep—pray for me, then
call me out for this, and call out the land too for the lies we whisper
    one another. If my blood never sleeps, then leave me
        to my reverberations through these four beating rooms; if my blood
never sleeps, freedom must be a prayer of marching. My cousin says
    Pray by moving your feet and I feel how a rogue pulse can be the difference
        between a legacy and a longing.

Murmur

And now I run, miles a day, for my health; and now I am
a haunted house of scars; and now I always fear,
like too many men in my family, that I will die because
of my heart; I always fear, like too many Black men,
that a heart is not enough to keep me alive

Grandpa's Gavel

I am mad at the red shelf for how tenderly it holds
the finished wood of my grandpa's gavel because,
really, I am ashamed to hold it, afraid my hands don't
hold tenderness quite the same, so when I do gather
the sense to stand and face it, my palm unfurled

over the handle like a rain cloud, it's not lost on me
how I darken its sheen. I take it into my hand and
it's now 1959 and I'm in the room: NAACP gathered,
Grandpa pounding the sounding block to call
order—here, big decisions; here, activism

engrained into mallet and memory, and I am
mad again at how little I can see from my clouding
of the room. Getting in my own way is my best trick;
getting in Grandpa's way is a new trick I try
when I pry the gavel from him and now it's 1975

and I'm in his church watching righteousness rain down
from his every word so I bow low in the back pew and pray
to be less shadow here and more snow—yes, pray that I may
accumulate, not obfuscate; yes, I pray his prayers don't find me
here, unable to face him, his beautiful words, his heart so set

on justice. So I pick up his gavel once more and now
we are caught in a SoCal sunset, and time has wrinkled him,
and time has also brought me to be, and this time he doesn't
lift a gavel, but a grandson, his second one—does he second-
guess his life's work entrusted to this careful boy? Does he notice

the clouds gathering where the sun makes its exit? Do I notice,
as my hand moves for the gavel again, how tenderly he held me
as if *this* were inheritance, as if something in me spoke
carefully of a place to rest his soul? Is this why I can't lift it,
even now, even then? Is this why the curl of my hand around

the stained maple reminds me of a fist and recoil rips
through my veins? Pop, I want to be brave like you, but
even a taillight can kill these days; these days, the bullets
and bombs you dodged in church have followed us
to schools and streets and theaters and stores and squares

and it's like a cloud hangs over the world constantly
and I am just scared of holding this. The world eats me
alive and never knows it—could I ever have an ounce
of your courage? Could I face myself and all
the prayers you placed in me, raining over

a world awash in chaos? I take this gavel
and all I am is right here. I'm brave enough
to do that. I'm brave enough to be, for you,
a bridge, perhaps. You were called to be strong
so that I might be your tenderness, but

is this enough? Is this enough? A question I weigh
each time I grasp this gavel, each time I place it back
on the red shelf, each time I pass by with a clouded
heart hoping for release, hoping to get a grip, hoping
to lift you up one day just the way you deserve.

Why are all the flags at half-mast—

Wait—are they still in the grocery store
or have they moved to the movie
theater? Call the mosque, call
the synagogue, call the church.
I was just at the gym and you were
just at that restaurant the other night
and my son loves that nightclub and . . .

Wait—whose school was it today?
Should my daughter do her homework
tonight? Should we instead search
the dictionary for "troubled," or
"well-regulated"? In the morning,
can she tell her teacher what she learned
while the teacher counts and hugs
and shields her students?

Tomorrow, we will wash the sidewalks.
Tomorrow, we will plant flowers on campus.
Tomorrow, we will curl ribbons and practice
learning names and badges and smiles, all
the while wondering who could tell what
was happening between the firecrackers
of a new year and old liberty.

Wait—I'm sorry to bother you
but I have to ask: When was the last time
you noticed the flag all the way at the top
of the pole?

My heart is

the color *run*, a 10.5-sized organ
      double-timing the pavement. My heart is the color
of *description*, the color of *reports* and *dispatch* and *in the area*.

      My heart is the color *why did he run?* My heart is
the color of *the cop feared for his life*. My heart is
      the color cops see when they see fear.

My heart is the color of *gun residue found on his hands*
      mixed with *an empty clip found in his pocket*; the color of
stop blocking the highway and get a job!, a subtle shade of

if he was so innocent, he wouldn't have run.
      My heart is the color of *do what the police tell you
and you won't get shot*, which is to say my heart

      is the mud on the bottom of 10.5-sized
pieces of "evidence" in Ziploc bags.
      My heart is the color *privilege*, the color of

a massive mirror hung high above the city.
      My heart is a set of skeletons in a closet
swapping bones. My heart is the color of a ghost

      in a coffee shop revising the chapters of its own making.
My heart is the color of seventeen; the color of a city
      of gymnasts contorting themselves beneath

a mirror just right to make a Black kid's death
      look like his own fault.
The color of justice. A color just north of red.

      My heart is the color of his poem and its tragedy;
it's the color of tears only a mother can cry—
      the color a mirror makes when it breaks.

I cut a sprig from a rosemary plant

and two more sprigs bloomed; I cut one
of the new sprigs, and out came a thumb
a lot like mine; I cut the thumb, and out
spilled blood; I cut the blood and out came
a flag; I cut the flag and a firework emerged
with a smoldering fuse; I cut the firework
and the Bill of Rights came spilling out; I cut
the parchment and there appeared my face;
I cut my face and out came thumping my teenage heart;
I cut my heart and out came my mother's murmur;
I cut her murmur and a blade sliced back at me;
The blade cut my hand and my own blood spilled
into the rosemary pot; the blade cut the soil and Aquarius
sprang up and into the sky; the blade cut the Water Bearer
and a flood came down; the blade cut the flood
but the flood cut back, sharpening itself until
the blade and the water merged and became a needle;
I picked up the needle, poked it through my palm
and heard my father cry for the first time; I sewed and
sewed and sewed, but the thread kept cutting a hole
in my hand wider and wider, and it sang as the thread passed
through and the song was a heartbeat filling in the pauses
in between my own; I cut the thread and the hole closed,
and the crying stopped, and the water dried, and the only thing
left was this song—it cut me open; it made a subwoofer
out of my chest; even now when the doctor lays
the stethoscope on me she says there are two hearts
talking over each other.

Muck

If there is a thin blue line in this country, it must be a trip wire
        kept close and camouflaged to the earth. If there is a trip wire
                in this country, its tensile strength must be tuned to the tibia
of Black shins. If this country has such strength, it is shattered
        by the placing of hands on car, draw of gun, howl of fear
                that a body may be a weapon, no matter how prone or probed.
The truth is that the dispatch of a bullet has two momentums.
        The truth is that any two feet can be standing in the wrong place.
                There is a muck none of us knows what to do with, but some of us
get to scrape it from our boots. A thin blue line is all that separates.
        The road to good intentions is paved Black—I am
                just a lowly welcome mat at the end
of the road, or in a portico whose columns gleam golden
        in a setting sun's curtsy. I want to believe the back of a badge
                is also gold. I want to believe the blood leaking from it isn't
my brother's or sister's. If I put on a uniform, where can I scrape
        my feet? Who will wash them if they are blood-clodded? It seems
                you only need pearls to be acquitted—it seems your skin must
resemble pearls for this to work. I've read this syllabus, found this line
        curled along the thin blue of America: *His death was his fault.*
                Is the bridge to salvation built with the bones of Black folks? I refuse
to believe Freedom's door lies at the end of a loved one's wounds,
        or that its knob turns in your reddened hands alone. Does it matter
                to you if I say Black bodies or Black lives, if all I am to you
is a good place to put your feet? Nothing will stop you,
        it seems. Nothing seems more American than raking muck
                from your boots, then stepping by.

Pardon

If my friends knew how much I danced
in the shower, they'd judge me—pardon me,

Earth, for all the water I've wasted—pardon
me for the spit in my mouth I give back

to make up for it. I've been told to make amends
when possible. The side effect is this heart

of mine caught up in shrinking and growing—
pardon, groaning—pardon, gloating. This is why

I dance in the water, to make joy something
precarious—pardon, precious—to learn to love

the threat of slipping, of losing balance.
If my friends knew that I can never throw away

sentimental things without kissing them goodbye,
they'd laugh about me—pardon, laugh at me—

and give names to anything I touch.
How do we learn shame for our little rituals?

Everyone I know walks backward out of dark
rooms and basements because we all know

haunters—pardon me, monsters—that make us
shudder. We are the strength we practice.

I practice writing poems not meant for prophet—
pardon, profit—pardon, private. I don't go to mass

but privately I do the sign of the cross sometimes
when I need grounding, when I need to hold on.

There's this earthquake I keep in my pocket I pray
I never show anyone; I'm okay letting myself

get torn apart—pardon, in part, because I might
deserve it. If my friends knew that I haven't always

been a good man, I wouldn't bother asking
them to pardon me—arrogance and freedom

are close cousins of mine. I have this little ritual:
recalling all the "last times" I didn't realize

were lasts at the time—full hands, a full heart,
kisses that weren't farewells, the echo of heat

that is thunder. Maybe I am what I fear
follows me out of the dirt—pardon, dark.

I fear I am an earthquake. I fear when I crack,
the earth will tell you from above and below.

A Second Opinion

1619. 1776. 1865. Because of these, I am.
        A rope rocks empty in the wind somewhere
                in Sumter because it never loved me. Maybe
life is all fire and parlor walls—still I go on
        dreaming of writing a Green Book for the stars;
                take me to Mars, tie my tongue in tectonics, then
let me be redshifted into oblivion. This much I believe:
        The future doesn't have a price (yet); a place is not
                who owns it; no book will make you love me.
1955. 1965. 1987. My heart is the space between
        boom-bap, dap, and desperation. Sometimes I dream
                of a Blacker me, and I know it is a dream because I can't
see faces clearly in dreams but I know a nesting doll
        just like I know the panic of a dream ending from its rush
                and repetition. The night sky and the Earth go on lying
back and forth to each other and from where I sit
        between them, I learn that stubbornness won't make me
                love me either. 1996. 2001. 2012. A road runs north
from Langdon because it desperately wanted me to be.
        This much I know: A place is more than its truth; some
                people have always known freedom; they aren't
the only ones fit for it.

Because

for Afton

I've always been better at word games;
because my sister has always been better
at mancala, her hand a shifty, surly,
scooping sidewinder dipping into
the pockmarked mahogany between us
at twelve and ten apiece, her hand a constant
passing back and forth around the board,
my hand shaped better for pen and paper;
because picking up pieces means knowing
where to place them; because we are pieces
of the people who came before us; because
ancestry is more Plinko than PAC-MAN,
yet this redistribution she is so good at,
like something in the blood, has made mine
boil watching her snatch away every last glob
of glass into the end pit, and I've marveled
at how easy it is for her to get there;
because it takes so much movement
to wind up where you're headed; because
mancala means *movement*; because she'd drop
her last stone in her store and say *Eat your heart out*
and I'd try in vain to prove her wrong
and always sow too short and fill the remaining
spaces with words I wasn't proud of; because
every game is still a word game to me, and I could
give the definition of *countenance* or easily spell
nauseous correctly on command, but I couldn't
seem to count my moves correctly, and isn't this
what family is for? Wasn't our blood picked up
and dropped here, moved all around this continent
just to arrive where we are? What's the word for that?
I'm asking because in the evening
of my youth, I'm only just learning that words
aren't everything; because even though these
childhood games are still fresh in my head, I still wish
for my sister to pick us up like little pieces of glass
and place us right back there.

Murmur

We are all ghost stories, silent chests, a heavy wager
of collapse, and isn't this what all our mothers fear?—
the fourth ghost: Every echo of love misplaced
somewhere deep in our hearts, reconvening over us
in our stillness, murmuring
Be careful.

Kill

It's the middle of the day in my life.
Not noon—middle; no, it's the first touch

       of fingertips to wax, a no-no that
       birthed the breakbeat I'll be buried in;

no middle ground in DNA double helix—
two staircases outstepping each other until

       no one knows what ground my deepest roots
       suck the soil of; no, the city is closed for work

today. No, a heart is not a place
to stay but a place to pass through

       I'm scanning the horizon
       where my sunset will catch,

even though my morning breath lingers
in lungs built for water; a "kill" is a body

       of water, so no more Black poets
       imagining their deaths; no more clouds pulling

damp dreams into this day; no old gods nor new.
I will be my own next ghost by November,

       when the fluke snowflakes sleet all December
       and January and—February knows not to fuck

with me anymore (I'm writing this so that I can
believe it); from my ribcage to my wrist, bass

       banging beneath the skin. It's the middle of the day
       there. Say it with me: I want a heart big enough

that I deserve; no, I want a big enough
heart; no, I deserve enough; no, I want

       the biggest heart; yes, I want what I deserve.

Systole, Diastole

I tell students all the time—I've never been great
    at math, but I do know this: Sometimes
knowing the value of X is the burden. Today
    I'm a C+ student caught on the quadratics

of a daydream, wondering if the sky is blue
    because grass took green, or why promises
keep like cotton candy in a rainstorm, or how
    even with all its stars America hasn't earned

its stripes. I struggle with plain math, too.
    Today the news said another man like me
was found hanging in a tree. The other day
    they showed a video of another man like me

being shot. They would have shown the woman like me
    being shot but the video went cotton candy. I got
just these five senses but I promise I've seen ghosts
    offering a better fate than blood or cuffs.

Today, when Malcolm tells me he was born late
    with his umbilical cord wrapped around his neck
I wasn't shocked. Everywhere there are nooses
    being tied, so why not within?

Better late than lynched. Today I set X equal to why
    my heart has four chambers and no room for forgiveness.
I've never been great at algebra, but I've learned to combine
    like terms: the thin blue of our atmosphere, the weight

of everything breathable bearing down on us, how little
    there is separating us from vacuum. I've learned to fear
this side of the sky and all its PSI. Today I'm seeing
    equals signs tilting like seesaws, wondering if in space

the opposite of pressure is liberty, whether emancipation
    is a synonym for weightlessness. Today my arteries
are storm drains full of sticky sweets, full
    of holding on, letting go, holding on,
letting go, holding on.

urmurmurmurmurmurmurmurmurmurmur
urmurmurmurmurmurmurmurmurmur
urmurmurmurmurmurmurmurmurmur
urmurmurmurmurmurmurmurmurmur
urmurmurmurmurmurmurmurmurmur
urmurmurmurmurmurmurmurmurmur
urmurmurmurmurmurmurmurmurmur
urmurmurmurmurmurmurmurmurmur
urmurmurmurmurmurmurmurmurmur
urmurmurmurmurmurmurmurmurmur
urmurmurmurmurmurmurmurmurmur
urmurmurmurmurmurmurmurmurmur
urmurmurmurmurmurmurmurmurmur
urmurmurmurmurmurmurmurmurmur
urmurmurmurmurmurmurmurmurmur
urmurmurmurmurmurmurmurmurmur
urmurmurmurmurmurmurmurmurmur
urmurmurmurmurmurmurmurmurmur
urmurmurmurmurmurmurmurmurmur
urmurmurmurmurmurmurmurmurmur
urmurmurmurmurmurmurmurmurmur
urmurmurmurmurmurmurmurmurmur
urmur   murmurmurmurmurmur
urmurmurmurmurmurmurmurmurmur
urmurmurmurmurmurmurmurmurmur
urmurmurmurmurmurmurmurmurmur
urmurmurmurmurmurmurmurmurmur
urmurmurmurmurmurmurmurmurmur
urmurmurmurmurmurmurmurmurmur
urmurmurmurmurmurmurmurmurmur
urmurmurmurmurmurmurmurmurmur
urmurmurmurmurmurmurmurmurmur
urmurmurmurmurmurmurmurmurmur
urmurmurmurmurmurmurmurmurmur
urmurmurmurmurmurmurmurmurmur

notes

The book's epigraph comes from the song "HEAVEN ALL AROUND ME" by Saba; the poem "Ghost Lessons" also borrows this song's lyric/title.

"Supreme" is written after Rickey Laurentiis.

"I was made fingerprint first" is written after Gregory Pardlo.

"Little Africa on Fire" is based on the photo *Little Africa on fire, Tulsa, Okla. Race riot, June 1st, 1921.*

"Breath" is inspired by the *Radiolab* podcast episode of the same name, which begins with a description of how fetuses receive oxygen while in the womb through a "trapdoor" in the heart.

"Black Holes" is inspired by a YouTube video by Vsauce.

"VY CMa" is inspired by a prompt from my former teacher Dawn Lundy Martin, and focusses (in part) on one of the largest stars ever observed/detected in the universe. The calculations are likely slightly imprecise, given that different sources provide different measurements of the star, the fact that the star pulsates, and that over years of drafts of this poem I have revised both the figures and scope of the calculations multiple times.

"The Pipe Bearer" was originally commissioned by The Frick Pittsburgh as an ekphrastic piece in conversation with the exhibit *Victorian Radicals* in early 2022. The poem is written after and takes its name from *The Pipe Bearer* by John Frederick Lewis.

"New Fruit Humming" borrows lyrics from the Iron & Wine song "Low Light Buddy of Mine."

"Working for the City" is after Hsia Yü.

"Pericardium" is a double golden shovel with beginning and end words borrowed from lines in the final stanza of M. Soledad Caballero's poem "Relics" from her book *I Was a Bell*.

"If my blood never sleeps" is titled after Ángel García's poem "Teeth Never Sleep."

"My heart is" is written after William Evans, and in memory of Antwon Rose Jr.

"Muck" is written in memory of Terence Crutcher.

"Because" is written after Todd Boss.

"Kill" is written after Lucie Brock-Broido.

Murmur **Playlist**: While working on this book, the following songs were in heavy rotation during my writing sessions. As a playlist, they are aesthetically and emotionally representative of the tone and mood of the book at various points. I invite you to listen to these songs before, during, or after reading *Murmur* (contains explicit lyrics, but if you've read this far, this shouldn't be surprising):

- o "HEAVEN ALL AROUND ME" – Saba
- o "Peace/War" – Shad
- o "Conrad Tokyo" – A Tribe Called Quest
- o "YSIV" – Logic
- o "Kool Aid & Frozen Pizza" – Mac Miller
- o "Smile Back" – Mac Miller
- o "LIFE" – Saba
- o "DNA." – Kendrick Lamar
- o "Under Pressure" – Logic
- o "Ode to Brooklyn" – Ohmega Watts

acknowledgments

Thank you to the editors of the following journals and anthologies in which some of these poems and previous versions of them first appeared: *A Little Gray Building, Basement Outpost, The Fourth River (Black Visions: A Jeffery "Boosie" Bolden Anthology), IDK Magazine, Kestrel, Laurel Review, The Minnesota Review, The Pittsburgh Neighborhood Guidebook, Pretty Owl Poetry, Rattle, Southern Indiana Review, Superstition Review,* and *TriQuarterly.*

I hold deep gratitude for so many people that naming them all here would be longer than this book, but I will try to be thorough and concise.

To my love and partner in life, Anna Weber. This book would not be possible without your unending support. Every day, you remind me that a life built on words and books is a life well spent—and I love what we've built. I love you to the moon (and not back).

To my family: Dad, Mom, Dylan, and Afton—everything I am today I owe to you. I am so grateful to live my life with you, and I love you with all my heart. And thanks to my cousins and family near and far, especially those who provided their generous time and care in hours of interviews with me: Bebe, Milton, Tony, and Lark. I forever treasure your words and your stories.

Thank you to those who helped to read, blurb, and shape this book, especially: Laura Brun, M. Soledad Caballero, Stephanie Cawley, Chris Graham, Laura Jones, Deesha Philyaw, Monica Prince, Nina Sabak, KG Strayer, Carrie Wittig, and Michael Yalch. A special thank you to my poetry brother Malcolm Friend: Your influence is all over this book, from the concept and the structure to your readership and motivation to pursue it—Popeye's and poems for life.

Thank you to all my friends who have grounded me and been there for me, especially the A-Team. And thank you to my students (past and present) at Falk and elsewhere, who help me to remember the power of words for play and introspection alike.

Thank you to the institutions that have supported me and my work with the space, time, and means to write this book, especially the University of Pittsburgh, Chatham University, the Pittsburgh Foundation, and the Heinz Endowments.

Thank you to my editor Mike Good for all your work and guidance; to Christine Stroud for believing in this book; and to my friend Melissa Dias-Mandoly for the beautiful layout and cover design.

A nod to the book *Heart: A History* by Sandeep Jauhar, which I read early in conceiving the project for this book.

This book began with travel, research, and oral interviews with family elders about their history and lived experiences as Black people growing up and living in America. Conducted from the fall of 2019 up through the emergence of the COVID-19 pandemic in the spring of 2020, this work was made possible by a 2019 Investing in Professional Artists Grant from the Pittsburgh Foundation and the Heinz Endowments.

new and forthcoming from autumn house press

Murmur by Cameron Barnett

Ghost Man on Second by Erica Reid
Winner of the 2023 Donald Justice Poetry Prize,
selected by Mark Jarman

Half-Lives by Lynn Schmeidler
Winner of the 2023 Rising Writer Prize in Fiction,
selected by Matt Bell

Nest of Matches by Amie Whittemore

Book of Kin by Darius Atefat-Peckham
Winner of the 2023 Autumn House Poetry Prize,
selected by January Gill O'Neil

Near Strangers by Marian Crotty
Winner of the 2023 Autumn House Fiction Prize,
selected by Pam Houston

Deep and Wild Places: One Life in West Virginia by Laura Jackson
Winner of the 2023 Autumn House Nonfiction Prize,
selected by Jenny Boully

Terminal Maladies by Okwudili Nebeolisa
Winner of the 2023 CAAPP Book Prize,
selected by Nicole Sealey

For our full catalog please visit: http://www.autumnhouse.org